Bridal Shower

_____

_____

_____

_____

Name

Favourite memory you have of the bride?

Advice you have for the bride-to-be?

Name

Favourite memory you have of the bride?

Advice you have for the bride-to-be?

Name

Favourite memory you have of the bride?

Advice you have for the bride-to-be?

Name

Favourite memory you have of the bride?

Advice you have for the bride-to-be?

Name

Favourite memory you have of the bride?

Advice you have for the bride-to-be?

Name

Favourite memory you have of the bride?

Advice you have for the bride-to-be?

Name

Favourite memory you have of the bride?

Advice you have for the bride-to-be?

Name

Favourite memory you have of the bride?

Advice you have for the bride-to-be?

Name

Favourite memory you have of the bride?

Advice you have for the bride-to-be?

Name

Favourite memory you have of the bride?

Advice you have for the bride-to-be?

Name

Favourite memory you have of the bride?

Advice you have for the bride-to-be?

Name

Favourite memory you have of the bride?

Advice you have for the bride-to-be?

Name

Favourite memory you have of the bride?

Advice you have for the bride-to-be?

Name

Favourite memory you have of the bride?

Advice you have for the bride-to-be?

Name

Favourite memory you have of the bride?

Advice you have for the bride-to-be?

Name

Favourite memory you have of the bride?

Advice you have for the bride-to-be?

Name

Favourite memory you have of the bride?

Advice you have for the bride-to-be?

Name

Favourite memory you have of the bride?

Advice you have for the bride-to-be?

Name

Favourite memory you have of the bride?

Advice you have for the bride-to-be?

Name

Favourite memory you have of the bride?

Advice you have for the bride-to-be?

Name

Favourite memory you have of the bride?

Advice you have for the bride-to-be?

Name

Favourite memory you have of the bride?

Advice you have for the bride-to-be?

Name

Favourite memory you have of the bride?

Advice you have for the bride-to-be?

Name

Favourite memory you have of the bride?

Advice you have for the bride-to-be?

Name

Favourite memory you have of the bride?

Advice you have for the bride-to-be?

Name

Favourite memory you have of the bride?

Advice you have for the bride-to-be?

Name

Favourite memory you have of the bride?

Advice you have for the bride-to-be?

Name

Favourite memory you have of the bride?

Advice you have for the bride-to-be?

Name

Favourite memory you have of the bride?

Advice you have for the bride-to-be?

Name

Favourite memory you have of the bride?

Advice you have for the bride-to-be?

Name

Favourite memory you have of the bride?

Advice you have for the bride-to-be?

Name

Favourite memory you have of the bride?

Advice you have for the bride-to-be?

Name

Favourite memory you have of the bride?

Advice you have for the bride-to-be?

Name

Favourite memory you have of the bride?

Advice you have for the bride-to-be?

Name

Favourite memory you have of the bride?

Advice you have for the bride-to-be?

Name

Favourite memory you have of the bride?

Advice you have for the bride-to-be?

Name

Favourite memory you have of the bride?

Advice you have for the bride-to-be?

Name

Favourite memory you have of the bride?

Advice you have for the bride-to-be?

Name

Favourite memory you have of the bride?

Advice you have for the bride-to-be?

Name

Favourite memory you have of the bride?

Advice you have for the bride-to-be?

Name

Favourite memory you have of the bride?

Advice you have for the bride-to-be?

Name

Favourite memory you have of the bride?

Advice you have for the bride-to-be?

Name

Favourite memory you have of the bride?

Advice you have for the bride-to-be?

Name

Favourite memory you have of the bride?

Advice you have for the bride-to-be?

Name

Favourite memory you have of the bride?

Advice you have for the bride-to-be?

Name

Favourite memory you have of the bride?

Advice you have for the bride-to-be?

Name

Favourite memory you have of the bride?

Advice you have for the bride-to-be?

Name

Favourite memory you have of the bride?

Advice you have for the bride-to-be?

Name

Favourite memory you have of the bride?

Advice you have for the bride-to-be?

Name

Favourite memory you have of the bride?

Advice you have for the bride-to-be?

Name

Favourite memory you have of the bride?

Advice you have for the bride-to-be?

Name

Favourite memory you have of the bride?

Advice you have for the bride-to-be?

Name

Favourite memory you have of the bride?

Advice you have for the bride-to-be?

Name

Favourite memory you have of the bride?

Advice you have for the bride-to-be?

Name

Favourite memory you have of the bride?

Advice you have for the bride-to-be?

Name

Favourite memory you have of the bride?

Advice you have for the bride-to-be?

Name

Favourite memory you have of the bride?

Advice you have for the bride-to-be?

Name

Favourite memory you have of the bride?

Advice you have for the bride-to-be?

Name

Favourite memory you have of the bride?

Advice you have for the bride-to-be?

Name

Favourite memory you have of the bride?

Advice you have for the bride-to-be?

Name

Favourite memory you have of the bride?

Advice you have for the bride-to-be?

Name

Favourite memory you have of the bride?

Advice you have for the bride-to-be?

Name

Favourite memory you have of the bride?

Advice you have for the bride-to-be?

Games

Bride or Groom

1. Who asked who on a date?

2. Who said I love you first?

3. Who initiated the first kiss?

4. Who is the first to admit they are wrong?

5. Who is the funny one?

6. Who is the romantic one?

7. Who is more messy?

8. Who is more likely to cry at the wedding?

9. Who is the better cook?

10. Who is the better driver?

How well do you know the bride?

1. What is her middle name?

2. Where was she born?

3. How did she meet the groom?

4. What was her first job?

5. What is her favourite song?

6. What is her favourite food?

7. Who is her celebrity crush?

8. What is her star sign?

9. What is her drink of choice?

10. What is her favourite movie?

The groom said what?

1. What is her ideal date? _____
_____

2. Where did you have your first kiss? _____
_____

3. What does he think is your worst habit? _____
_____

4. What does he love about you? _____
_____

5. What three words would he use to describe you? _____
_____

The groom said what?

6 Where did you have your second date?_____

_____

7. What is her biggest pet peeve?_____

_____

8. What is the one thing she can't live without?_____

_____

9. What nickname do you have for each other?_____

_____

10. What was his first impression of you?_____

Paper bride

Guests divide into teams, one member from each team is the model, the rest of the team have to create a wedding dress using toilet roll and place on the model.

Guess the couple

Print out pictures of celebrity couples, ask the guests to name the couple. The more obscure the better.

Wedding Charades

Each guest has to act out a wedding themed movie and the rest of the guests have to guess what the film is. Movie ideas, Mamma Mia, The Wedding Singer, 27 dresses, Bridesmaids, My Big Fat Greek Wedding.

Guess the love song

Play a snippet of 10-20 love songs and your guests need to write down the name of the song and artist who sings it.

Two truths and a lie

Each of the guests introduce themselves and tell three experiences they have had with the bride, two of the statements are true, the other is a lie, the rest of the guests need to guess which is the lie.

Create your own cocktail

Ask each guest to create their own cocktail, with the bride being the judge of the best one.

Gift Log

Name	Gift

Name	Gift

Name	Gift

Name	Gift

Name	Gift

Name	Gift

Name	Gift

Name	Gift

Name	Gift

Name	Gift

Name	Gift

Name	Gift